LET YOUR LIGHT SHINE

Celebrational Poetry
for the Inner Spirit
Inspired by Natasha Lewis

William H. Lewis III

OliWil Publishing

Copyright © 2020 by William H. Lewis II
Los Angeles, California
All rights reserved
Printed and bound in the United States of America

Published by OliWil Publishing
Los Angeles, California 90062
Email: oilwilpublishing@gmail.com

Cover Design / Logo Design / Photograph of the Author:
Plans Prints & Designs
Cover Image: John Towner on Unsplash

ISBN: 978-1-7344901-1-4
10 9 8 7 6 5 4 3 2 1
First printing: September 2020

No part of this book may be reproduced, stored in a retrieval system or transmitted in any form or by means without the prior written permission of the publisher-except by a reviewer who quotes brief passages in a review to be printed in a newspaper, magazine, or journal.

For inquires contact: oilwilpublishing@gmail.com

Acknowledgments for
"Let Your Light Shine"

First, I would like to thank God for His unconditional love, blessings, mercy, grace, and peace. I could not be me without You, Father God. I love You with my whole heart.

To my late, great sister, the beautiful Ms. Natasha LaFrance Lewis. Truly, I would not be the man I am today without your unconditional love, nurturing, guidance, support, encouragement, kindness, wisdom, and one-of-a-kind personality. Natasha, you blessed and enriched my life in so many ways, and I will be forever grateful to you. Although you're no longer with us physically, I feel your spirit and impact every day of my life. Natasha, thank you for everything! I will love you forever, and I will honor you every chance I get. Rest well with your heavenly Father. You are truly in great hands. God bless you, Natasha.

To my beautiful and amazing wife, Mrs. Cynthia Lewis. Babe, I thank God for your life. Babe, thank you for being the best wife, mother, friend, helper, motivator, supporter, and nurturer I could have ever hoped and prayed for. God predestined our love and union before the foundation of this world and for that, I thank Him. Babe, you make me whole, content, and strengthen me in so many ways. Thank you for all that you do, and for being the backbone and pillar of our beautiful family.

To our beautiful and amazing children, Olivia and William. What a great and tremendous blessing you have been. I can't thank God enough for blessing us so greatly. Olivia and William, I love you with every fiber of my being. Such smart, intuitive, energetic, loving, caring, thoughtful, and sweet kids. Olivia and William, always know God is always with you, and He loves you unconditionally. There is nothing God can't do. God will never leave nor forsake you. God's love will never run out. God bless you, as you continue to grow, learn, develop, explore, and teach. Daddy will always love you and want nothing but the best and greatest for you.

To my first great teachers, my parents, Mr. William H. Lewis, Jr., and Ms. Ann D. Lewis. Mom and Dad, God blessed me with two of the best parents. I treasure, admire, respect, and love you unconditionally.

Mom, you have been a constant source of strength, support, unconditional love, and fervent prayers. Mom, you have overcome great obstacles and setbacks, but by God's grace and mercy, have persevered. I truly thank God for your life, and that He chose you to be my mother.

Dad, thank you for always being there for me. Even through your darkest hours and most difficult times, your role as a father

Acknowledgments

never wavered. God has always been on your side, and I thank Him for that. Thank you, Dad, for your wisdom, guidance, help, and prayers.

Mom and Dad, I love you so much; I can never repay you for what you have been in my life. God bless you both.

To my brother, Cedric Lewis. We have been through so much together. We have had good and difficult times, but God never left our side. Cedric, thank you for being a true big brother. You protected, nurtured, guided, and shaped me in many ways, and for that I thank you. God bless you, as you have endured your share of trials and tribulations, but have displayed true resilience, fight, grit, and have persevered. Not because of, but in spite of. God bless you and your wonderful family always.

Last, but certainly not least, my good brother and true friend, Mr. Lovell Williams. My good brother, what a great blessing you have been in my life. There are not too many people in this world like you. Humble, God-fearing, caring, loving, empathetic, patient, gifted, kind, thoughtful, helpful, and an all-around great human being. Lovell, thank you very much for your vision, diligence, hard work, dedication, attention to detail, desire, and willingness to help me bring this very special and important project to life. I truly could not have done it without you my good brother and friend.

May God continue to bless you and your beautiful family in every area of life. I love you brother, and I truly thank God for your life.

Table of Contents

Introducing "Let Your Light Shine" 9

Greeter 13

Sisters 14

Made Everything Better.. 16

Storyteller 17

Hospitable 18

The Light of the World (Matthew 5: 14-16)................. 19

Difference Maker 20

Children of God 21

In Charge of Wardrobe 22

Beautiful 24

Foundation 25

Always There 26

Aspirations 27

Auntie Tasha 29

Family Photos 31

Psalm 23: "The Lord is My Shepherd" 33

Brothers 34

Fight of Your Life 35

Legacy 36

In the Arms of God 37

Typical Natasha 38

Missing My Sister 39

Sheep 41

Matthew 25:31-46 43

Ready or Not 45

1 John 3:11-24 47

Pictorial Blessed by God 49

Introducing
"Let Your Light Shine"

On September 6, 2019, the life I had known for almost 47 years changed dramatically forever. This was the day my beloved sister, Ms. Natasha LaFrance Lewis, transitioned out of this world. It was extremely difficult to comprehend, but it was more difficult to process such a monumental loss. You see, my sister Natasha was 10 years older, which meant she existed before I came into the world, and had lived a life without me. But it was the total opposite for me because from the day I came home from the hospital, and up to the last day I saw my sister alive, she had always been there. Even when Natasha left home at the age of 20, she was never absent from my life. Natasha was my everything. She nurtured, loved, shaped, comforted, guided, and molded me into the great man I am today. Natasha and I also shared a special bond that was predestined by God. We had our own language, and would often laugh hysterically. What a great sister. What a great blessing.

Natasha was more than just a great sister, she was a true beacon to the world, and changed lives in a very profound and powerful way. Natasha loved everyone wholeheartedly, regardless of their background. She had an infectious smile and personality that dispelled any depths of darkness, sadness, or disappointment. Speaking of smiles, I recently read a quote that said, "Let your smile change the world; never let the world change your smile." I found this thought-provoking quote to be emblematic of Natasha the person, and how she lived her life in this world.

As bright as Natasha's smile permeated throughout our lives, there were some difficult moments of heartache, heartbreak, loneliness, sadness, physical and emotional pain, and mental anguish. As well as grief, shock, and dread. As her loving brother and one of her biggest supporters, I will never fully understand what my sister went through. I will never know all of the things she internalized. I will never know what was going through my sister's mind during her final hours. I will never know my sister's innermost thoughts because Natasha put everyone before herself. Natasha made sure everyone around her was okay even when she was not, and when you're that person that represents joy, happiness, laughter, and a sense of humor, everyone leans on you.

Natasha never wanted to appear vulnerable or down, because this was not the way people perceived her. Which brought about a lot of pressure, and it often made it difficult for Natasha to open up and reveal her true feelings. It wasn't until the very end that I had the chance to see my sister open up and express her true feelings, emotions, and pain. Unfortunately for my sister, the physical damage was already done. Hindsight is 20/20, and if I had known then what I know now, I would have done everything possible to help my sister get better. I know a God that sits high and looks low and has all power in His hands. God created Natasha for a specific purpose, and when she fulfilled her God-given purpose, He called her home. Where she could be free of pain, hurt, stress, anxiety, distress, and physical trauma. God knew Natasha before He created her, as was stated in Jeremiah 1:5: "Before I formed thee in the belly I knew thee; and before thou camest forth out of the womb I sanctified thee, and I ordained thee a prophet unto the nations."

Greeter

There is nothing like a warm and welcoming smile
There is nothing like a sincere and heartfelt embrace
There is nothing like coming into the house of God and
kindness, love, and joy meets you at the door
It's a great feeling
It does something wonderful to the soul
It invigorates the spirit
God preordained Natasha to be a greeter
God put something special in Natasha
God put peace in Natasha
God put unconditional love in Natasha
God put the Holy Spirit in Natasha
Natasha was blessed to hold this priceless
position for many years
Natasha encouraged the children of God to come back
week after week, and they did
God bless all the church greeters of the world

Sisters

Natasha was blessed by God with sisters who loved
her unconditionally
Sisters she had known for many years
Some she met in elementary
Some she met in junior high
Some she met in high school
But regardless of where they met, she was
always there for them
and they were always there for her
They shared a special bond that carried them through
good and difficult times
And when one sister was down, the other
sisters would pick her up
They prayed together
They laughed together
They cried together
They struggled together
They persevered together
They traveled together
They celebrated milestone birthdays together
They celebrated class reunions
Class of "80" in the house
They celebrated family reunions

Let Your Light Shine

They celebrated weddings
They mourned together
And when their sister Natasha transitioned out of this world, they came together to celebrate her in the most honorable way
Thank you sisters for always having Natasha's back
I know how much you loved her
And I know how deeply she loved and cared about all of you

Made Everything Better

Natasha made life better in so many ways
Her one of a kind personality made the difference
Her Million dollar smile made the difference
Her organic sense of humor made every situation memorable
And if you were blessed enough to spend some time with her, laughter was always on the menu
Her kindness and generosity was truly authentic
And she always wanted everyone to be comfortable
She always wanted everyone to have a great time

Storyteller

Natasha told stories better than anyone
Detailed orientated
Always animated
She painted vivid pictures which made you feel present
in the story
And Natasha always had a story to tell
"Y'all ain't gone believe what happened"…
"When I tell you…"
Whether it was about church, work, going out with
friends, or the celebrities she would
run into occasionally
And no one could embellish a story like Natasha
Truly one of a kind

Hospitable

"I'll fix your plate"
"Would you like another bottle of water?"
"I got you some more napkins"
"I already packed you some food to take home"
"Just relax, I got you"
These are the friendly, caring, kind, warm, and sincere words of Natasha
Whether you were a guest at her place or somewhere else, Natasha's hospitality never changed
She always took care of everyone else first
She would clean up
She would wash dishes
She would sweep
Natasha was just that kind of person
She left a lasting impression
She was the epitome of selflessness

"The Light of the World"
Matthew 5: 14-16

14 Ye are the light of the world. A city that is set on a hill cannot be hid.
15 Neither do men light a candle, and put it under a bushel, but on a candlestick; and it giveth light unto all that are in the house.
16 Let your light so shine before men, that they may see your good works, and glorify your Father which is in heaven

Difference Maker

Hard working
Dedicated
Valuable
Punctual
Passionate
Detail oriented
Energetic
Mentor
Teacher
Counselor
Confidant
Committed
Natasha was one the hardest working
people that I had ever known
She added so much to every employer
Regardless of her title
Regardless of her position
Natasha did not have a college degree
She possessed something far more important, people skills
She was a true leader that led by example

Children of God

Love thy neighbor as thyself
Love one another
God is love, and love is God
God commanded us to love one another
God never commanded us to be perfect
We are all children of God, and we were made in his image
Natasha treated the children of God with love and respect
The way God intended
She did this to the best of her ability
She never met a stranger
She did what was necessary to be a blessing to her
brothers and sister in Christ

In Charge of Wardrobe

What a blessing it is to celebrate a
birthday of any kind
But milestone birthdays take on a different meaning of
significance
God has blessed our family to experience multiple
milestone birthday celebrations
Natasha was truly built for milestone birthdays
I believe she missed her calling as a "Milestone birthday
coordinator"
I mean she organized everything
Literally everything
But when it came to wardrobe, Natasha was
strictly business
When our beautiful mother turned 65, Natasha made it
clear that everyone was wearing
blue jeans and white collared shirts
There were no exceptions!!!!!!
And we could not use the excuse
"I don't have blue jeans or white collared shirt"
Natasha would ask you your size, and
would buy the clothes for you

Let Your Light Shine

She would buy different styles of jeans and shirts just in
case there was a conflict in taste
Natasha was not playing!!!
At all!!!
There will never be another
Natasha LaFrance Lewis
Period!!!

Beautiful

Not because you were my sister
Not because you were the best sister ever
Not because you loved me unconditionally
Not because you were always there for me
Not because you had my back one million percent
Not because you were selfless
Not because you were so generous
You were beautiful because of your spirit
You were beautiful because of your heart
You were beautiful because of your soul
You were beautiful inside and out
No one could dress like you
No one had your style
No one had your grace
No one had your one of a kind smile
God only made one you

Foundation

Three generations
Grandmother, mother, and granddaughter
Grandmother set the example for mamma
Mamma set the example for daughter
That's the way the cycle of life goes
Natasha was no different
Natasha was blessed to have spent priceless time with her maternal grandmother that was affectionately known as "Madea"
Madea was kind, giving, loving, caring, God fearing, hospitable, and was known to house people that were homeless
Madea was also strong, tough, and was willing to protect her family at all cost
Natasha inherited many of her traits and characteristics from Madea
And just the same, our beautiful mother is loving, caring, generous, kind, God fearing, hospitable, and empathetic
Mamma is also strong, fearless, and tough when necessary
Both of these great women loved Natasha unconditionally and was instrumental in shaping the great woman we came to know and love
Thank you God for the solid foundation of madea and mamma

Always There

As far back as I can remember, Natasha was always there
Through the good and bad
Through the highs and lows
Natasha was always there
Even when she wasn't there in person, Natasha was always just a phone call away
Even when she moved out of the house at the age of 20, Natasha was still there
Regardless of the occasion or situation, Natasha was there
When our daughter was born, Auntie Tasha was there
When our son was born, Auntie Tasha was there
I would find out later that Natasha checked herself out of the hospital hours before
Though sick and not in the best of health, Auntie Tasha was there
My sister was willing to sacrifice her own life, to be present for the birth of her nephew
Organically selfless
This is why I love and miss my sister so much!

Aspirations

We are all born for a specific purpose
Some people realize their purpose early in life
While others discover their purpose much later
We also have goals and dreams
Some people reach their goals
Some people realize their dreams
Natasha had goals
One of her goals was to be a police officer
Natasha's passion for law enforcement was great
She talked about it frequently
She pursued her passion full throttle
She had wonderful stories to tell about her experience in the academy
But unfortunately it never materialized
How unfortunate
Natasha would have made an incredible police officer
Natasha loved people
Natasha cared about people
Natasha was empathetic
Natasha was God fearing
Natasha was stern when necessary
Natasha was a natural leader
Natasha was understanding
We need these traits in our world more than ever

William H. Lewis III

Natasha also wanted to be a foster care parent
Natasha loved and adored children
Children held a special place in her heart
And she spoke vehemently about becoming a foster parent
weeks before her transition
God bless his children that aspire to be great

Auntie Tasha

I cannot think of a person that loved being an aunt more than Natasha
She embraced this title with the greatest love and care
She never took being called auntie for granted
She loved it
She relished it
And I will never forget the day when my wife and I gave her the news that she was going to be an aunt
She screamed
She yelled
She cried
She rejoiced
She was in total euphoria mode
And before that day, she would always throw not so subtle hints
Every Christmas up until 2013, Natasha would give us onesies as gifts
With phrases such as "It's a boy" It's a girl" or I'm an aunt"
It was the funniest thing ever
It was the cutest thing ever
I knew how much my sister wanted to be an aunt
Our heavenly Father knew too
God answered her prayers
God answered her fervent prayers

And when my wife and I announced her second pregnancy, it was another memorable moment

My wife and I decided to do the gender reveal on father's day 2017 with our families in attendance

The anticipation was extremely high

Given the fact that we already had a beautiful daughter

And when the blue confetti came out, no one got it

Well except auntie Tash

I just remember her screaming "It's a boy!" "It's a boy!" "It's a boy!"

It was pandemonium!

This was one of Natasha's favorite words by the way

  And auntie Tasha was on cloud 1000 that great and memorable day

Family Photos

Priceless memories
A moment in time
Reflections
Rewind
Looking at old family photos is like reading a good book
It becomes truly engaging and it takes you away from the present times and into the times of old
Recently I was looking at photos from our childhood
I must say that every picture brought a bright smile to my face
Sure we had our ups and downs just like any other family, but overall we enjoyed some good times
Looking at photos of Christmas morning for example
Smiles
Laughter
Gift wrapping paper galore
The sun shining through the pitcher window in the living room
And I can't forget about Easter Sunday
Dressed up nicely
Color coordinated (So that's where Tasha got it from)
Easter baskets in hand
Mom and dad took very good care of us
"Those were the best times" my dad said as I studied each and every photo

Dad was right
It was the best time because there was no pressure
No personal drama
No worries
No problems
Just being young and innocent
Truly enjoying our lives as children
And these were some of the best times of Natasha's life
Drill team
Playing the flute in her junior high school orchestra
They even did a record
Cheerleading
Hanging out with her girls
Just having the time of her life
Talking on the phone (Constantly)
I thank God for our family photos
I thank my mom for keeping our family photos in tact

Psalm 23
"The Lord is My Shepherd"

1 The Lord is my shepherd; I shall not want.
2 He maketh me lie down in green pastures: he leadeth me beside the still waters.
3 He restoreth my soul: he leadeth me in the paths of righteousness for his name's sake.
4 Yea, though I walk through the valley of the shadow of death, I will fear no evil: for thou art with me; thy rod and thy staff they comfort me.
5 Thou preparest a table before me in the presence of mine enemies: thou anointest my head with oil; my cup runneth over.
6 Surely goodness and mercy shall follow me all the days of my life: and I will dwell in the house of the Lord forever.

Brothers

Brothers
Brothers
Brothers
God fearing brothers
Loving brothers
Caring brothers
Thank you brothers for respecting Natasha
Thank you brothers for being there for Natasha in good and difficult times
Thank you brothers for always having Natasha's back
Thank you brothers for praying with and for Natasha
Thank you brothers for standing tall for your sister Natasha
Thank you brothers for loving Natasha unconditionally
Thank you brothers for coming together to celebrate Natasha at her home going service
Thank you brothers for your strength, love, comfort, and support
God bless and keep you brothers

The Fight of Your Life

My sister was one of the strongest people I had ever known
A fighter
Resilient
Perseverant
Never
Never
Never give up attitude
But life happens to all of us
No one is exempt from the trials and fire of life
No one is exempt from the hurt and pain
No one is exempt from being overwhelmed by life
But we push forward to the best of our ability, and that's what Natasha did
Natasha continued to be present despite her physical struggles
But at times the pain was too much
Nevertheless, Natasha continued to fight
Natasha would often say "I'm fighting for my life" when faced with situations that were not worth her time and energy
Natasha wanted to save her energy for things that mattered
Natasha wanted to save her energy for moments that created new memories
I'm so proud of my sister for fighting to the end
I love you Tash
I will always love you

Legacy

Life is more than money
Life is more than materialism
Life is about inspiring our brothers and sisters in a profound and unforgettable way
Life is about pursuing the will of God for our lives
Natasha did everything in her power to make life better for her brothers and sisters
Thoughtful
Kind
Giving
Hospitable
Loving
Caring
Empathetic
Servant
Selfless
God fearing
Supportive
Protective
Humble
Helper
Personable
Faithful
Compassionate
This is the true legacy of Natasha Lewis

In the Arms of God

Finally free
Free from the cares of this world
Free from the hurt and the lies
Free from the disrespect and dishonesty
Free from the physical pain
Free from the sleepless nights
Free from sadness
Free from the constant flow of tears and unhappiness
Free from smiling to make others feel comfortable
God has you now
God's love is unconditional
God's love is everlasting
God is peace
God is rest
God is truth
God is absolute
God is everything that you never found consistently on earth
God is eternity
God is the King of Kings
God is the Lord of Lords
Natasha, God has prepared a place for you

Typical Natasha

Thoughtful and selfless to the very end
The day my sister transitioned from this world, will go down as one of the darkest and most painful days of my life
But my sister would bring a smile to our faces on that fateful day
The day before her passing, Natasha stopped by the store to pick up snacks
She bought the snacks for the repast of one of her sister's that preceded her in death
In my sister's possession were chips, water, candy, and other snacks
Those of us at the hospital that fateful day, laughed and smiled momentarily
We laughed and talked about how Natasha was still thinking of her brothers and sisters
She did not allow the physical pain to deter her from being the person God created her to be
Thank you Tash for giving us something to laugh about one last time
Thank you Tash for giving us something to laugh about on one of the saddest days ever

Thank you
Thank you
Thank you
I love you Tash

Missing My Sister

Still in shock
Still in disbelief
I wake up everyday thinking about my sister
I think back to all of those moments God allowed us to have
Whether good or sad
Whether delightful or difficult
At least I had my sister
I miss her unique and unforgettable smile
I miss her loud knee slapping laugh
I miss her love
I miss her support
I miss her kindness
I miss her thoughtfulness
I miss her powerful presence
I miss her hospitality
I miss talking to my sister
I miss calling my sister
I miss texting my sister
I miss her good food
I just miss her so much
My sister left a void that will never be filled or replaced
But truly one of the most saddest things about losing my sister, is that she will not be at the hospital for the birth of our third child
Auntie Tasha will never get the chance to meet her baby nephew

William H. Lewis III

This is beyond heartbreaking
Our son will never get the chance to meet his auntie Tasha
But he will definitely be acquainted with her spirit
He will know her through all of us
He will know that she was here
I know that on that special day, auntie Tasha's spirit will permeate throughout the hospital room
Her larger than life personality and smile will be on full display
Thank you God for the life and legacy of my beloved sister; Ms. Natasha LaFrance Lewis
And to every person that has ever lost a sibling and or siblings, may the love and peace of God comfort and strengthen you forever!

Sheep

There is nothing like a peace of mind
There is nothing like understanding
There is nothing like transparency
There is nothing like clarity
A few weeks after we buried my beloved sister, there were some unanswered questions about her final moments at the hospital
My family and I needed answers to those questions
I reached out to the hospital, and they were extremely, empathetic, kind, professional, and helpful
My mom and I met with the Quality Control Manager and other hospital staff
The Quality Control Manager went over everything with us line by line
Though it was beyond difficult, my mom and I by God's grace endured to the end
We now had a better understanding about my sister's final moments of life
But I must say that God works in mysterious ways
You see, our plans will never be in alignment with God's plans
Because our mission that day was to get clarity and understanding, but God sent my mom and I there to get a word
At the end of our meeting, the Quality Control Manager wanted to know more about Natasha the person
And we told the Quality Control Manager how selfless,

thoughtful, kind, loving, caring, empathetic, helpful, giving, and humble Natasha was, and that she helped everyone
The haves and the have nots
And with the biggest smile on his face, the Quality Control Manager said "Natasha was a sheep"
Then he asked us if we thought we would see Natasha again, and we said yes!
He encouraged us to read Matthew 25:31-46
Not only was the Quality Control Manager and his staff warm and welcoming, he sent us home with these encouraging words from the Lord:

Matthew 25: 31-46

31 When the Son of man shall come in his glory, and all the holy angels with him, then shall he sit upon the throne of his glory:

32 And before him shall be gathered all nations: and he shall separate them one from another, as a shepherd divideth his sheep from the goats:

33 And he shall set the sheep on his right hand, but the goats on the left.

34 Then shall the King say unto them on his right hand, Come, ye blessed of my Father, inherit the kingdom prepared for you from the foundation of the world:

35 For I was an hungered, and ye gave me meat: I was thirsty, and ye gave me drink: I was a stranger, and ye took me in:

36 Naked, and ye clothed me: I was sick, and ye visited me: I was in prison, and ye came unto me.

37 Then shall the righteous answer him, saying Lord, when saw we thee hungered and fed thee? or thirsty, and gave thee drink?

38 When saw we thee a stranger, and took thee in? or naked, and clothed thee?

39 Or when saw we thee sick, or in prison, and came unto thee?

40 And the King shall answer and say unto them, Verily I say unto you, inasmuch as ye have done it unto one of the least

of these my brethren, ye have done it unto me.

41 Then shall he say also unto them on the left hand, Depart from me, ye cursed, into everlasting fire, prepared for the devil and his angels:

42 For I was an hungered, and ye gave me no meat: I was thirsty, and ye gave me no drink:

43 I was a stranger, and ye took me not in: naked and ye clothed me not: sick, and in prison, and ye visited me not.

44 Then shall they also answer him, saying, Lord, when saw we thee an hungered, or athirst, or a stranger, or naked, or sick, or in prison, and did not minister unto thee?

45 Then shall he answer them, saying, Verily I say unto you, Inasmuch as ye did it not to one of the least of these, ye did it not to me.

46 And these shall go away into everlasting punishment: but the righteous into life eternal.

Ready or Not

Losing my only beloved sister was not only painful and devastating, but a wake-up call
I never envisioned my sister dying
I only envisioned my sister living
But God has a day for all of his children
No one is exempt
Regardless of socioeconomic status
Regardless of social class
Regardless of race
Because death does not discriminate
Death will not wait for God's children to get it together
We have to get it together now
We have to love one another now
We have to forgive one another now
We have to bless the less fortunate now
We have to help the homeless now
We have to fight racism now
We have to fight injustice now
We have to fight poverty now
We need prison reform now
We need to show kindness now
We need to show gratitude now
We need peace now

William H. Lewis III

We need understanding now
Let's not waste time on nonsense
Let's not waste time on things that are counterproductive
The clock is ticking
The clock never stops ticking
Let's not take life for granted
Let's not take our gifts for granted
Let's not take God's calling on our lives for granted
Let's not take God's purpose for our lives for granted
Let's appreciate one another
Let's celebrate one another
Let's love one another in the way God intended
God commanded us to love one another

1 John 3: 11-24

11 For this is the message that ye heard from the beginning, that we should love one another:

12 Not as Cain, who was of that wicked one, and slew his brother, And wherefore slew he him? Because his own works were evil, and his brother's righteous.

13 Marvel not, my brethren, if the world hate you.

14 We know that we have passed from death unto life, because we love the brethren. He that loveth not his brother abideth in death.

15 Whosoever hateth his brother is a murderer: and ye know that no murderer hath eternal life abiding in him.

16 Hereby perceive we the love of God, because he laid down his life for us: and we ought to lay down our lives for the brethren,

17 But whoso hath this world's good, and seeth his brother have need, and shutteth up his bowels of compassion from him, how dwelleth the love of God in him?

18 My little children, let us not love in word, neither in tongue; but in deed and in truth.

19 And hereby we know that we are of the truth, and shall assure our hearts before him.

20 For if our heart condemn us, God is greater than our heart, and knoweth all things.

21 Beloved, if our heart condemn us not, then have we confidence toward God.

22 And whatsoever we ask, we receive of him, because we keep his commandments, and do those things that are pleasing in his sight.

23 And this is his commandment, That we should believe on the name of his Son Jesus Christ, and love one another, as he gave us commandment.

24 And he that keepeth his commandments dwelleth in him, and he in him. And hereby we know that he abideth in us, by the Spirit which he hath given us.

Pictorial Blessed by God

William H. Lewis III

Let Your Light Shine

William H. Lewis III

Let Your Light Shine

William H. Lewis III

Let Your Light Shine

Let Your Light Shine

William H. Lewis III

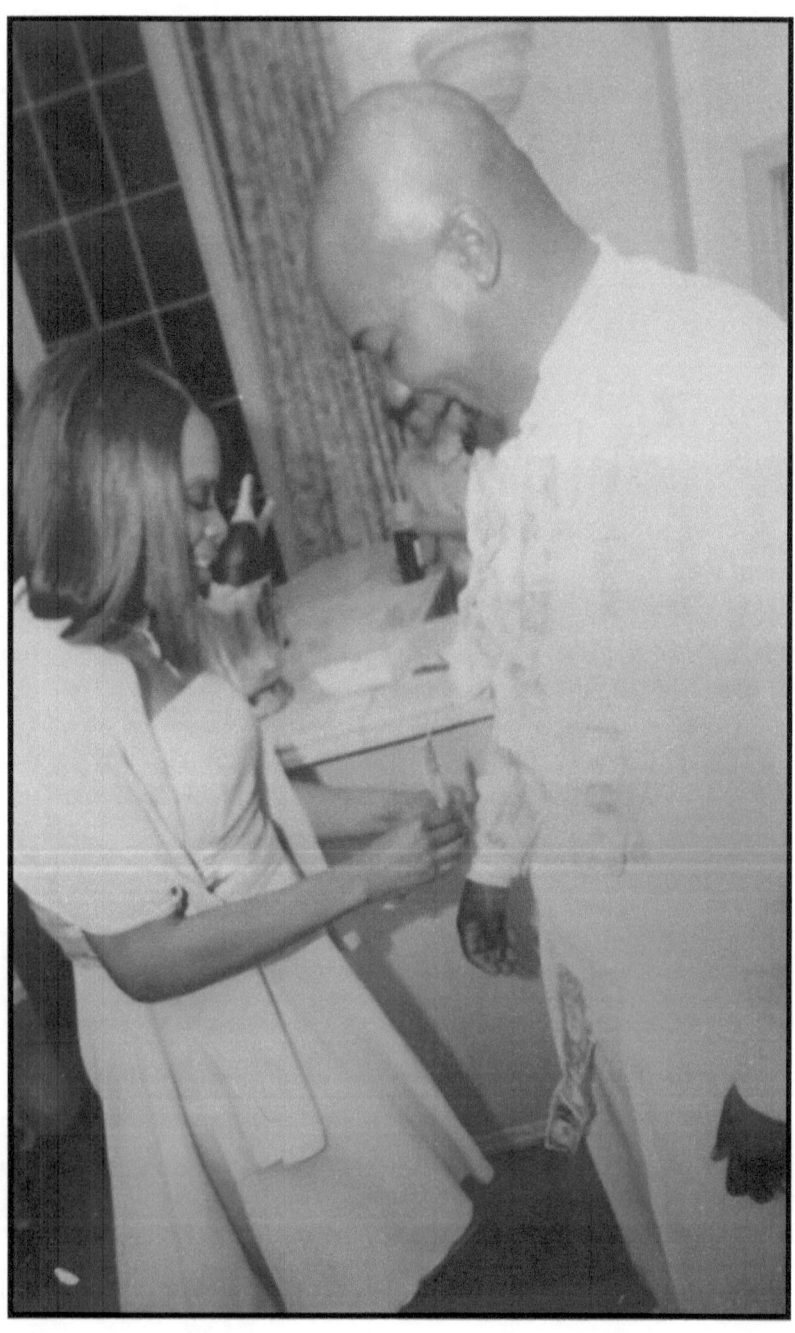

Let Your Light Shine

William H. Lewis III

Let Your Light Shine

William H. Lewis III

Let Your Light Shine

William H. Lewis III

Let Your Light Shine

Let Your Light Shine

www.ingramcontent.com/pod-product-compliance
Lightning Source LLC
Chambersburg PA
CBHW021123080526
44587CB00010B/616